PUFFIN B

READY TEDDY
GO

Are you ready?
Are you teddy?
Then go for this exciting
Koalection of the funniest,
most unBEARable, teddiest jokes
around. All of them chosen to
PANDA to your honeybone!

Other books by Shoo Rayner

**THE CHRISTMAS STOCKING JOKE BOOK
SANTA'S DIARY**

Picture books

**VICTORIA, THE WEDNESDAY MARKET BUS
LAMB DROVER JIM
MY FIRST PICTURE JOKE BOOK**

READY TEDDY GO

by
SHOO RAYNER

PUFFIN BOOKS

PUFFIN BOOKS

Published by the Penguin Group
Penguin Books Ltd, 27 Wrights Lane, London W8 5TZ, England
Viking Penguin, a division of Penguin Books USA Inc.
375 Hudson Street, New York, New York 10014, USA
Penguin Books Australia Ltd, Ringwood, Victoria, Australia
Penguin Books Canada Ltd, 2801 John Street, Markham, Ontario, Canada L3R 1B4
Penguin Books (NZ) Ltd, 182–190 Wairau Road, Auckland 10, New Zealand

Penguin Books Ltd, Registered Offices: Harmondsworth, Middlesex, England

First published 1991
1 3 5 7 9 10 8 6 4 2

Text and illustrations copyright © Shoo Rayner, 1991
All rights reserved

The moral right of the author/illustrator has been asserted

Printed in England by Clays Ltd, St Ives plc
Filmset in Monophoto Times

Except in the United States of America,
this book is sold subject to the condition
that it shall not, by way of trade or otherwise,
be lent, re-sold, hired out, or otherwise circulated
without the publisher's prior consent in any form of
binding or cover other than that in which it is
published and without a similar condition
including this condition being imposed
on the subsequent purchaser

Did you hear about the cute teddy with the turned-up nose?
Every time she sneezed her hat blew off!

What is the difference between a teddy bear?
One of his legs is both the same!

You remind me of the sea.

Because I'm wild, reckless and romantic?

No, because you make me sick!

THE TEDDY BEARS' PICNIC

How do you start a milk-pudding race?
Sago.

What is that fly doing on the ice-cream?
Learning to ski!

Is that roast pork or an old radio?
I don't know, but it's got a lot of crackling!

What do elves have for their tea?
Fairy cakes.

What do you call a train full of sweets?
A chew chew train!

What do you call a rich rabbit?
A million hare!

You've got such a sweet face . . .
. . It's just like a humbug!

What do drivers have in their sandwiches?
Traffic jam!

Is that smoked salmon?
Not yet it isn't!

What do you call a cow eating grass?
A lawnmooer!

What do you get if you cross a cow with a camel?
Lumpy milk shakes!

Why do cows have bells?
Because their horns don't work!

What happens if you walk under a cow?
You get a little pat on the head!

Where do milk shakes come from?
Nervous cows!

What game do cows like to play at birthday parties?
Moosical chairs!

If you want to run fast eat runner beans.

What is a hedgehog's favourite food?
Prickled onions!

What's long and green and goes hith?

A thnake with a lithp!

What flies and wobbles?
A jellycopter!

Did you hear the story about the biggest cake in the world?
It's very hard to swallow!

Don't eat with your knife.
But my fork leaks!

What's worse than a maggot in your apple?
Half a maggot in your apple!

What dance do tin cans do?
The cancan, of course!

"I've only got one sandwich."

"Hold on – I'll cut it in two!"

I'd like a honey sundae
with chocolate sauce,
loads of chopped nuts
and a scoop each of
vanilla, pistachio
and raspberry ripple
ice-cream.
Would you like a cherry on the top?
Goodness no!
I am on a diet, you know!

Can I eat honey
with my paws?
*No, eat your paws
separately like
everyone else!*

Eat up your honey. It's good for growing bears.
But I don't want to grow bears!

How did you get that bump on the head?
I got hit by a tomato.
But tomatoes are soft.
Not when they're still in their cans!

I know a bear who lives on garlic alone.
I'm not surprised he lives alone if all he eats is garlic.

I'll have a hamburger, please.
With pleasure!
No, just pickle and tomato sauce, thanks!

Why have these
potatoes got
buttons on them?
*Because they're
jacket potatoes!*

How do you get an electric shock?
Eat a current bun.

What do you call a collection of bopping buns?
A bun dance!

He's a spring onion!

WHAT WOULD YOU CALL A BEAR...

Who drives a truck?
LAURIE.

Who wears a raincoat?
MAC.

Who doesn't have much hair?
FREDBARE.

Who's been stitched up?
SEW AND SEW.

Who's been buried for a hundred years?
PEAT.

Who can put up shelves?
ANDY.

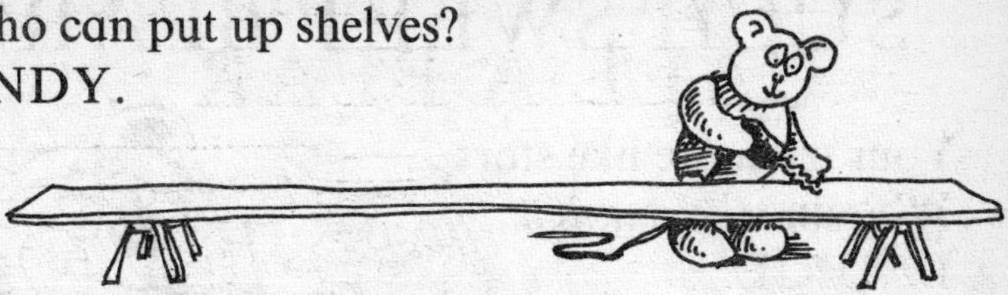

Who can paint?
ART.

Who floats in water?
BOB.

Who has a wooden head?
EDWOOD.

Who has three wooden heads?
EDWOOD WOODWOOD!

SUCH SWEET BEARS

Your teeth are like stars . . .
They come out at night!

Your hands are like petals . . .
Bicycle petals!

Your skin is like a peach . . .
A football peach!

Your eyes are warm,
soft and brown . . .
Like mud!

Your ears are like flowers . . .
Cauliflowers!

Why do you play so much football?
Oh, just for kicks!

Why is a football pitch so wet?
Because the players keep dribbling!

How do you stop your nose from running?

Stick out your foot and trip it up!

DOCTOR, I FEEL SICK

Doctor, I think I'm turning into a cuddly teddy bear.
When did you first notice this complaint?
Ever since I stopped being a flopsy, wopsy bunny!

"Doctor, doctor, I think I need some change in my life."

"Take twenty pence three times a day!"

Why was the Egyptian teddy so confused? *Because his daddy was a mummy!*

"Mummy?"

Since I've only got one eye, can I have a half-price TV licence?

Why are you standing
in that bowl of water?
*The doctor said
I should take these
pills in water,
three times a day!*

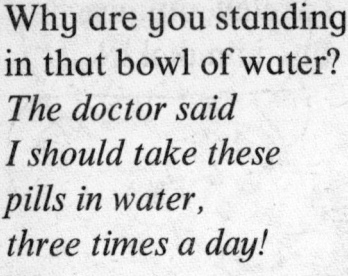

What's the best
cure for flat feet?
A foot pump.

How did you get that splinter in
your finger?
I scratched my head.

I've not felt well since I had some beans yesterday.

Did they look all right when you opened the tin?

Oh! Was I meant to open the tin?

The doctor said I should take these pills on an empty stomach...
I did, but they kept rolling off!

AATCHOO!

Sneeze a jolly good fellow!

Doctor, I think
I'm changing
into a frog.
*Well, go and
do it in the
croakroom!*

What do you call
a Chinese cold?
Kung flu!

Doctor, I can't
stop myself from
stealing things.
*Oh good! Can you
get me a new car?*

I bumped into
Teddy yesterday.
*Was he pleased
to see you?*
No, we were both
in our cars at
the time.

I just had the stuffing
knocked out of me.
Have you got any scars?
No, I don't smoke.

Doctor, I think I've got fleas.
You must be hopping mad!

"You're a nit!"

Change of Address

Mr & Mrs Louse
have moved to

Edward Bear
Scratch End
Itching-in-the-Fold

Please come to our
Louse-warming party
next Wednesday

"Fleas a jolly good fellow!"

DOCTOR: I think you may need glasses.
PATIENT: *Why's that, doctor?*
DOCTOR: That's the wardrobe, the door is over there!

I think I've got a bearway.

What's a bearway?

About a hundred kilos.

I think I've got a matterbaby.

What's a matterbaby?

Nothing really, but it's nice of you to ask!

GONE FISHING

Why are you fishing over the side of that bridge?
I'm waiting to catch the next bus that comes along.

What do you get if you jump in the river?
Wet!

How do you make a waterfall?
Throw it out of the window!

That pond isn't very deep. The water only comes half-way up the side of those ducks!

Why are you doing the backstroke?
Because I didn't want to swim on a full stomach!

Quick! Quick!

You've got Quick-ups!

ADDING UP

Think of a number, double it and add three thousand two hundred and forty-six.

Multiply the answer by one million, seven hundred and twenty-six thousand, nine hundred and forty-two. Then divide by three.

Now take away the number you first thought of and what do you get?

The wrong answer!

If two's company and three's a crowd, what is four and five?
Why, four and five are nine, of course!

Which snakes are good at arithmetic?
Adders.

Which insects are good at adding?
Arithmeticks.

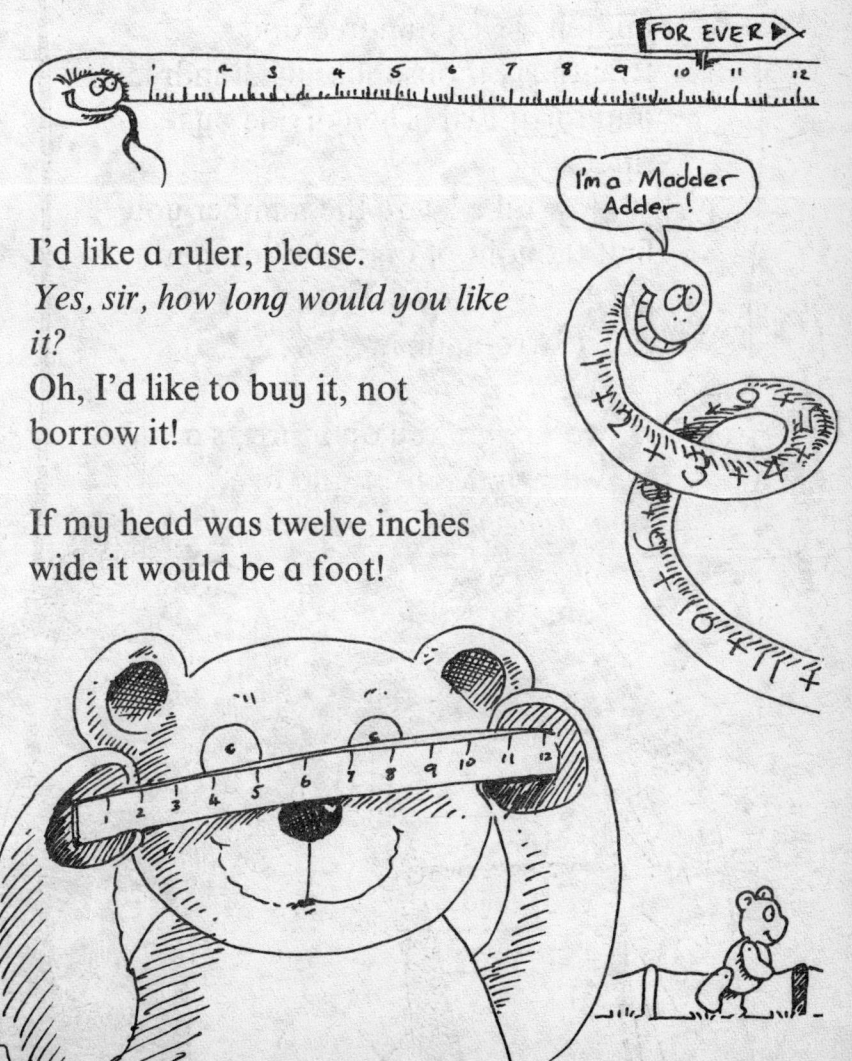

Adder, not Ladder!

FOR EVER

I'm a Madder Adder!

I'd like a ruler, please.
Yes, sir, how long would you like it?
Oh, I'd like to buy it, not borrow it!

If my head was twelve inches wide it would be a foot!

Round and round the... Two step & tickle you.

Tree's a jolly good fellow

One step... Garden, like a Teddy Bear... under here!

Shall I put the kettle on?
No, I quite like the dress you're wearing!

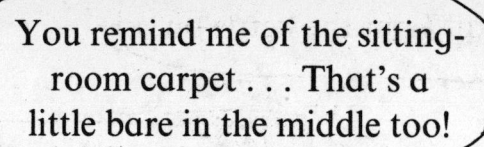

You remind me of the sitting-room carpet... That's a little bare in the middle too!

Knock, knock.
Who's there?
Yvonne.
Yvonne who?
Yvonne to be alone!

Knock, knock.
Who's there?
William.
William who?
William mind your own business!

Knock, knock.
Who's there?
Euripedes.
Euripedes who?
Euripedes trousers
so get me another pair!

Shoo Box

Knock, knock.
Who's there?
Amos.
Amos who?
A mosquito bit
me on the bottom!

My nose runs and my feet smell.
Then you must be upside down!
Sniff
Sniff
Sniff
Sniff

I choose all my own clothes.
Oh, the dog chews all of mine!

Which animal do you look like when you're in the bath?
A little bare!

If my nose grows any longer it will be a foot!

What do you have at the top of your leggies?
Hippies!

Where does a general keep his armies?
Up his sleevies!

Did you know that your legs have got a bottom at the top?

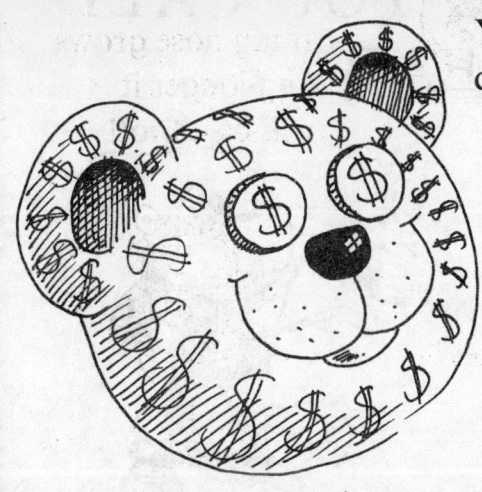

Your face looks like a million dollars...
It's all green and crinkly!

I'd like a brown fig-leaf to match my eyes, please.
Sorry, sir, we haven't got a brown one, but we've got a soft one to match your head!

It's a cover up!

WHAT DO YOU CALL A BEAR...

Who is a barber?
A hair bear.

With no clothes on?
A bare bear.

Who is a stunt man?
A dare bear.

Who didn't get on
the netball team?
A spare bear.

Who is hard to find?
A rare bear.

Who needs sewing up?
A tear bear.

Who goes up and down?
A stair bear.

What do you call a family of French bears?
Mère Bear, père Bear and frère Bear.

REAL BEARS

What do you call
a really friendly
grizzly bear?
*A complete
failure!*

What do you call
a really nasty
grizzly bear?
Sir!

Why do grizzly bears have fur
coats?
*Because they'd look pretty stupid
in anoraks!*

What do you do if a grizzly bear eats your biro?
Chew your pencil instead!

I can play the piano by ear!
So what! I can fiddle with my whiskers.
unBEARable Music!
FIN

Take that bear out of this house. It's full of fleas!

I wouldn't go in there if I were you. Mum says it's full of fleas!
Knock

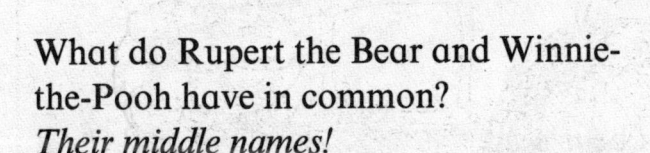

Have you ever hunted bear?
No, but I've been fishing in my shorts!

What do Rupert the Bear and Winnie-the-Pooh have in common?
Their middle names!

Eat up your porridge and you'll grow up to be a beautiful girl.

Didn't you eat yours when you were young then?

What's the difference between an American grizzly bear and an Australian koala bear?
Two continents and the Pacific Ocean!

What is a bear's favourite drink?
Koka-Koala!

How do you know if a panda's been in a fight?
Because he'll have two black eyes.

What happened to the bear who ran away with the circus?
The police made him bring it back!

Why shouldn't you take a bear to the zoo?
Because he'd rather go to the movies!

So you got arrested for feeding the bears at the zoo, did you?
No, I got arrested for feeding the bears to the lions in the zoo!

The Great Bear lost the race to the stars, but it did win a constellation prize!

Pole Star

Why is the Little Bear right on target?
Because it is a shooting star!

That star over there is Mars.

Then which one is Pa's?

He's looking through his TEDDY scope!

If you were walking through the forest and came upon a giant, snarling, hungry grizzly bear, would you carry on or run back to camp?
I'd run back to camp.
What, with a bear behind?

What is white and furry and smells of peppermint?
A Polo bear!

Why do you keep shaving off your fur like that?
Because I'm stuffing a cushion.

BABY TALK

Why are babies so full of happiness?
Because they have a nappy time!

Would you rather have a baby brother or a baby sister?
I'd rather have a jelly baby actually!

Just because he's a bouncing baby, it doesn't mean you can throw him out the window!

I think you must be
twelve years old,
because my brother
is six and he's
only half as mad
as you are!

How old are your grandparents?
*I don't know. We've had them an
awful long time though!*

How old are you? Eight.

And what are you going to be? Nine!

What a dummy!

FINISH

ART GALLERY
Blue Bear Picasso
Moaning Lizzy
Is this modern art?
No, madam, it's a mirror!

Dancing Bear Degas

Bear Garden

Polar Bear in a snowstorm

Cheese a jolly good fellow!

FINISH

BEDTIME

What is the first thing that you
do in the morning?
Wake up!

What is the last thing that you
do at night?
Go to sleep!

That teddy just rolled her eyes
at me!
*Well, pick them up and roll them
back again!*

Where's your alarm clock gone?
I threw it away. It kept on going off while I was asleep!

I can't get to sleep.
Well, sleep on the side of the bed and you'll soon drop off!

Why was teddy the toast of the town?
Because he forgot to turn off the electric blanket!

Where was teddy when the lights went out?
In the dark!

COP SHOP

If you found some money, would you keep it?
No, I'd spend it as soon as I could!

"I hope I didn't see you robbing that bank?"

"I hope you didn't see me too!"

I'm POLICED to meet you.

♪ POLICE a jolly good fellow.. ♪

What did the policeman
say to his tummy?
You're under a vest!

Do you have anything to say?

No, I just don't give a hoot!

He doesn't give a dicky-bird, my lud!

What did the robber say to the watchmaker?
I'm so sorry to take so much of your valuable time!

Who is the greatest detective in fairyland?
Sherlock Gnomes!

Ah ha! Sherlock Bones!

What does
CID
stand for?
Coppers In Disguise!

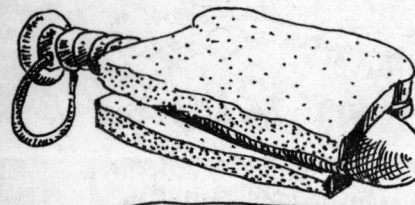

What does a policeman have in his sandwiches?
Truncheon meat!

That's never a police dog!

It's a plain-clothes police dog!

Why is that dog ticking?

He's a watch dog!

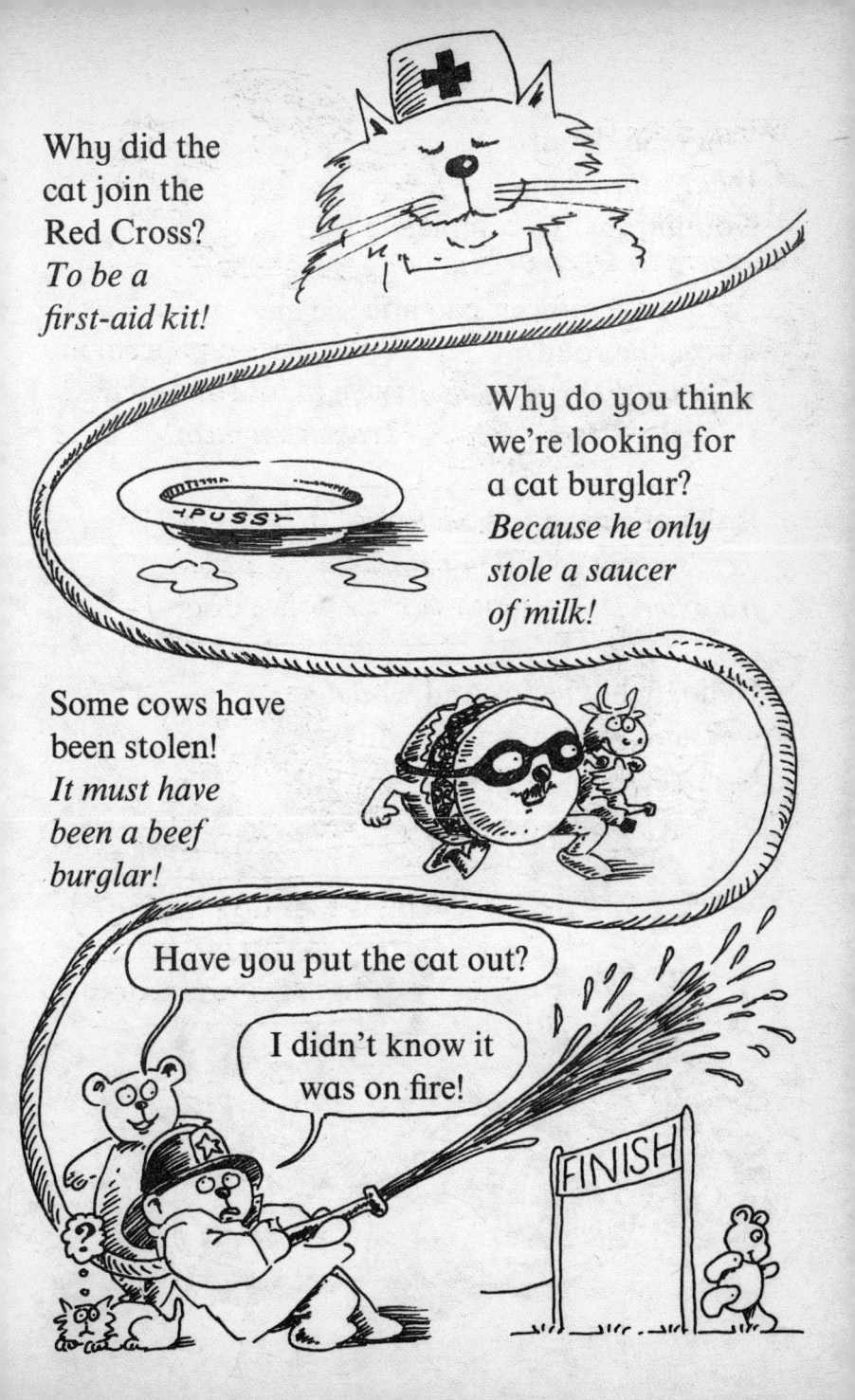

Why did the cat join the Red Cross? *To be a first-aid kit!*

Why do you think we're looking for a cat burglar? *Because he only stole a saucer of milk!*

Some cows have been stolen! *It must have been a beef burglar!*

Have you put the cat out?

I didn't know it was on fire!

You're under arrest!
What's the charge?
Nothing . . . It's completely free!

Excuse me, officer, can you see me
across the road?
*Wait until I've crossed over and
I'll wave if I can!*

Is this the road to London?
*Yes, sir, but I wouldn't start
from here!*

Hello, hello, hello! And who do
we think we are, sir, Speedy
Gonzales?
Si!

Speedy jolly good fellow!

Why are
policemen
so strong?
*Because they
can hold the
traffic up
with one hand!*

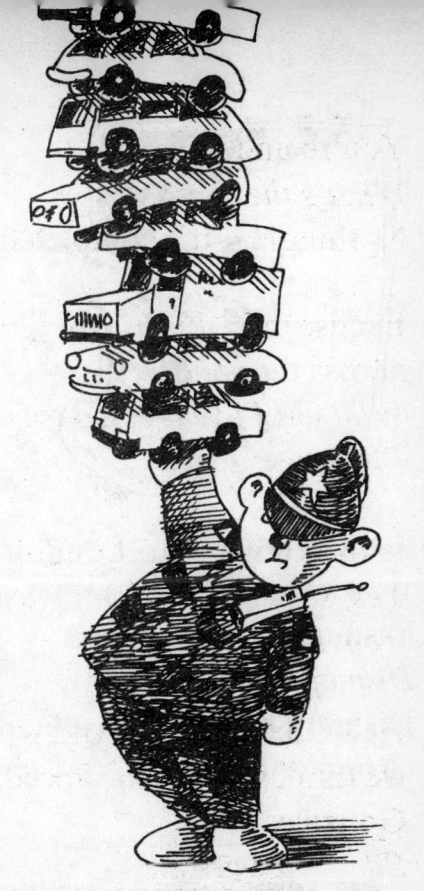

Knock, knock.
Who's there?
Elisa.
Elisa who?
Breath Elisa!
Would you like
to blow into
this bag, sir?

Excuse me, sir, why are you
driving in reverse?
*Because I know the Highway Code
backwards!*

Knock, knock.
Who's there?
Boo.
Boo who?
Oh, please don't cry!

Knock, knock.
Who's there?
Dismay.
Dismay who?
Dis may be the
wrong door!

Knock, knock.
Who's there?
Wood.
Wood who?
Wood who know
what time it is?

Knock, knock.
Who's there?
Isadore.
Isadore who?
Isadore on the
right way round?

Knock, knock.
Who's there?
Orange.
Orange who?
Orange you glad
it's not a great
big grizzly bear!

Knock, knock.
Who's there?
Cuck.
Cuck who?
That's the first
cuckoo of spring!

There was once a bear who got lost in the desert. He'd been wandering around for days in the heat and was very hungry and thirsty.

A bee flew by him. If I know anything about bees, it's that bees make honey, he thought.

So he followed the bee until he came to a canyon a mile wide and a mile deep. The bee flew over the canyon to the other side where, the bear could plainly see, was a pool of fresh water and a tree. In the tree the bear could just see a beehive and that could only mean honey!

How did the bear get across the canyon?

2 Bee or not 2 Bee!

Do you give up?
Don't worry, so did the bear!

BEES MAKE HONEY!

What goes zzub?
A bee flying backwards!

Why do bees hum?
Because they don't know the words!

If a straight line is the shortest distance between two points, then what is a bee line?
The shortest distance between two buzz stops!

I'm glad I don't like honey. If I did I'd eat it and I hate the stuff!

STUPID!

Said teddy, 'You know it is quite funny,
That whenever I'm eating some honey,
whatever I eat
goes straight to my feet
and never ends up in my tummy!'

Why are you dancing with that jar of honey?
It says twist to open!

Don't bee naughty, honey, just beehive yourself while I comb your hair!

SCARE BEARS!

What do you get
if you cross a
teddy bear with
a vampire?
*Something warm and
cuddly that bites
you on the neck!*

How does a vampire cross the
ocean?
In a blood vessel!

What do you call
a toothless vampire?
A silly old sucker!

Did you hear about
the toothless
vampire?
*He could give you
a nasty suck!*

MMMMMM! Love at first bite?

We're blood brothers!

When can you play a trick on a vampire?
On April Ghoul's Day!

What does a polite vampire say after he has bitten you?

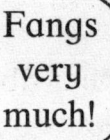

Fangs very much!

What do you call
a small vampire?
A pain in the knee!

Why are vampires so
simple-minded?
Because they're suckers!

What's a vampire's
favourite fruit?
A blood orange.

Where does a
vampire stay
when he's on
holiday in
America?
*The Vampire
State Building!*

Why are vampires crazy?
Because they are sometimes bats!

I used to be a Werebear but I'm all right nowwwwwww!

What is a monster's favourite party game?

Swallow my leader!

"I can see right through you."

"Try using spooktacles!"

What tunes do ghosts whistle?

"Haunting melodies!"

"You don't look well. You've gone as white as a sheet!"

"What's a Werebear?"

"Be quiet and comb your face!"

What does a polite monster say?

I'm pleased to eat you!

Pickled Organs

Bacon and Legs!

What do monsters like to eat?

Baked beings on toast!

WHAT DO YOU CALL A BEAR...

Who howls at the moon?
A WERE BEAR.

Who says naughty words?
A SWEAR BEAR.

Who's never around?
A SQUARE BEAR.

Who's in hiding?
A WHERE BEAR?

Who likes sewing?
THREAD BEAR.

Who has fleas?
A BUG BEAR.

Who sells tickets?
A FARE BEAR.

Who gives you bad dreams?
A NIGHT BEAR.

Who hides round corners?
A BEWARE BEAR.

Who is a handyman?
A REPAIR BEAR.

Did you know that you've got jelly in one ear and custard in the other?
Sorry, can you speak up, I'm a trifle deaf!

Why did the teddy bear cross the road?
Because he wanted to have a word or two with the chicken!

I much prefer long socks to short socks.
You know, I think I would agree with you on that one.
That's great . . . Do you prefer them boiled or fried?

I think I prefer them stewed!

Teddy walked into a bank with his seams torn open and his stuffing falling out . . . He'd gone to open a shavings account!

"Did you know that my ears are made of cloth and that my head is full of sawdust?"

"So am I. How about next Tuesday?"

"Time hangs so heavily on me these days."

"Well, why don't you get a lighter watch?"

How do you stop
a teddy bear race?

Say **FINISH!**

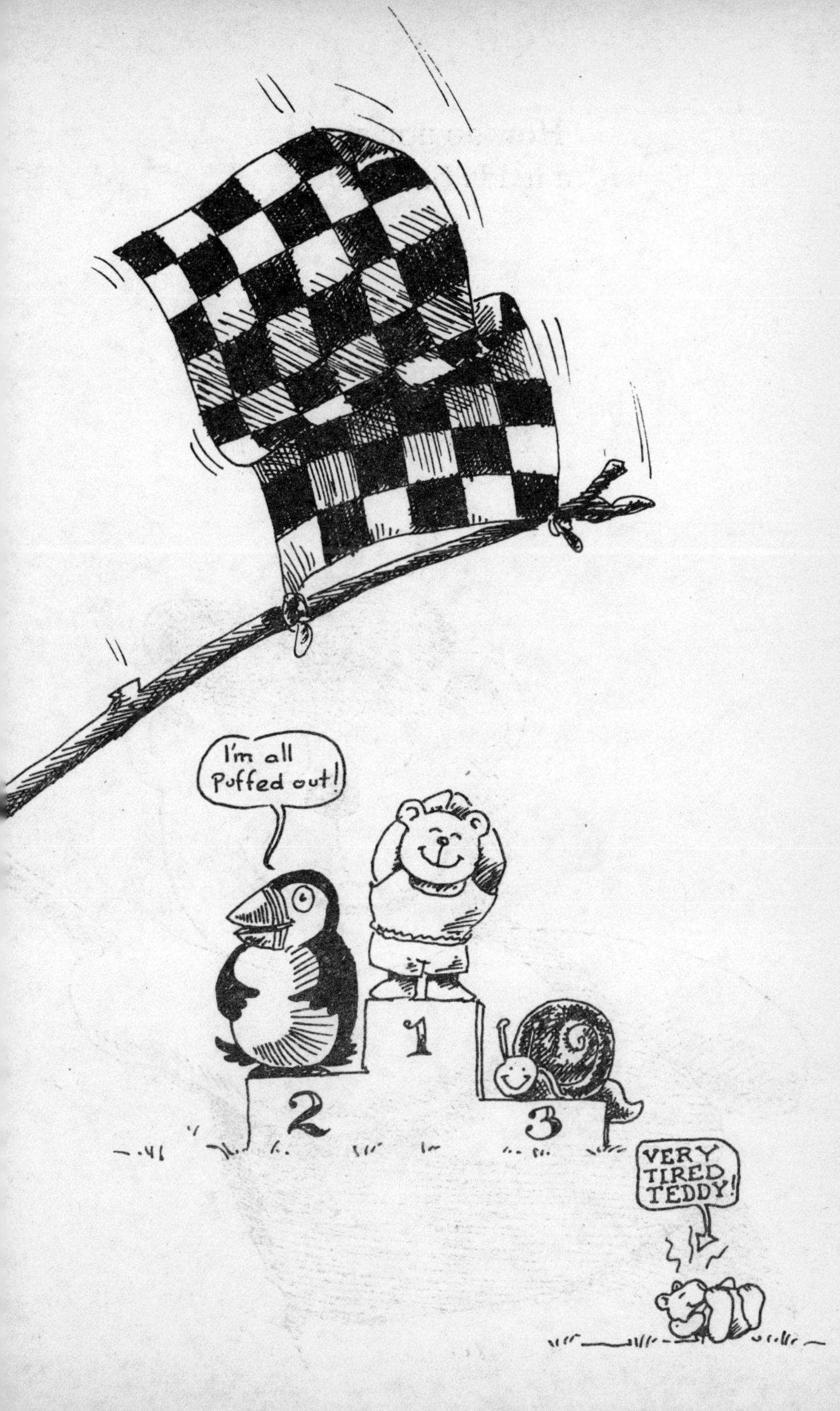
I'm all Puffed out!
1
2
3
VERY TIRED TEDDY!